AF405976

ANCIENT ROME

2nd Grade History Book
Children's Ancient History Edition

Speedy Publishing LLC
40 E. Main St. #1156
Newark, DE 19711
www.speedypublishing.com

Copyright 2015

All Rights reserved. No part of this book may be reproduced or used in any way or form or by any means whether electronic or mechanical, this means that you cannot record or photocopy any material ideas or tips that are provided in this book

Ancient Rome was an Italic civilization that began on the Italian Peninsula as early as the 8th century BC.

Ancient Rome was a powerful and important civilization that ruled much of Europe for nearly 1000 years.

Much of Ancient Rome's
history has had a lingering
effect on our world
today, and our citizens
have learned much
from their way of life.

CITTÀ DEL VATICANO
ROMA
OSTIA ANTICA
Albano L.
Genzano
Castel
Pomézia
Tor Valànica
di S. Lorenzo
Lido del Pini
Lavinio
Nett

Pescara
Roma
314
61
25
15
13
17
Arsoli
Tagliacozzo
17 M. sicana
13
A25
Avezzano
Anticoli
Corrado
Camerata Nuova
10
S i m b r u i n i
12
10
Capistrello
82
A10
15
16
Subiaco
M. Autore
1853
Luco
dei Marsi
16
24
48
M. Viglio
2156
M. Romecchia
1759
52
Olevano Romano
Campo Catino
1800
411
18
82
10
Genazzano
155
Giglio
11
14
M
Guarcino
Collepardo
Certosa
di Trisulti
15
13
14
19
Fiuggi
47
A1
11
17
16
155
Anagni
155r
6
24
155
Alatri
18
Segni
Ferentino
18
Veroli Casamari
9
Sgurgola
20
11
34
214
Frosinone
Sacco
13
Carpineto
Romano
17
9
19
Sora
M. Semprevisa
1536
22
Ceccano
19
12
19
22
Sermoneta
19
56
22
Arpino
Sezze
13
Roccagorga
156
Priverno
Amaseno
18
Fossanova
7
15
48
148
Sonnino
A u s o n i
45
85
Fondi

In the early 6th Century B.C., Rome first grew into power as a Republic. The Rome leaders were elected officials that served for a limited amount of time. They had a complex government with written laws, a constitution, and a balance of powers.

In 45 BC Julius Caesar took over the Roman Republic and made himself the supreme dictator. A few years later, Caesar Augustus became the first Roman Emperor and this was the start of the Roman Empire.

The city of Rome
was the capital city
of the civilization
of Ancient Rome.

The center of Rome had many other famous and important buildings like the Colosseum, the Pantheon, and Pompey's Theatre.

POSITIS SIGNIS ET
IVSSV CLEME

ONT · MAX · OPV

The Colosseum is an oval amphitheatre in the centre of the city of Rome, Italy. It was built during the Roman Empire. Construction on the Colosseum began under the emperor Vespasian in 72 AD, and was completed in 80 AD.

It was used for gladiatorial contests and public spectacles such as mock sea battles, animal hunts, executions, re-enactments of famous battles, and dramas based on Classical mythology.

Every Roman city had
a public bath where
people came to bathe and
socialize. Men and women
bathed at different
times or in different
areas of the baths.

The floors of the baths
were heated by a Roman
system called a hypocaust
that circulated hot air
under the floors.

The Pantheon was
originally built as a temple
to the gods of Ancient
Rome. The Pantheon is
the best preserved of
all Roman buildings.

The Pantheon's dome is still the world's largest unreinforced concrete dome. The Pantheon is the oldest standing domed structure in Rome.

AGRIPPA·L·F·COS·TERTIVM·FECIT

While Rome was the center of the empire, there were many large and important cities throughout the empire. The most important area of every Roman city was the forum.

The forum was a
gathering place of
great social significance,
and often the scene
of diverse activities,
including political
discussions and debates,
rendezvous and meetings.

The Romans are famous for keeping lots of written records. It was how they kept their large empire organized.

They kept records on every Roman citizen. They also kept written records of laws and decrees made by the government.

M · FIL · SEVE
CO · PONTI
IL · ANTON
O · P · TIM
STITVI

O PIO PERT
IC MAXIM
NO AVG P
S FORTISS
M IMPE

Pompeii was an ancient
Roman town-city. The
town was founded around
the 6th-7th century BC
by the Osci or Oscans.

In 79 AD, disaster struck the city when it was buried under 20 feet of ash and debris from the eruption of the nearby volcano, Mount Vesuvius.

Visit

BABY PROFESSOR
EDUCATION KIDS

www.BabyProfessorBooks.com
to download Free Baby Professor eBooks
and view our catalog of new and exciting
Children's Books

www.ingramcontent.com/pod-product-compliance
Lightning Source LLC
Chambersburg PA
CBHW081241130726

47997CB00009B/2956